SAFE · AND · HEALTHY · LIVING
REVISED EDITION

"

Spick and Span

The Health Parade

Growing Big and Strong

Safety Every Day

Doing Your Best for Health

Building Good Health

Helping the Body in Its Work

The Healthy Home and Community

"

SAFE · AND · HEALTHY · LIVING
REVISED EDITION

THE
HEALTH PARADE

BY

J. MACE ANDRESS, Ph. D.

Formerly Editor of School and Health Department in *Hygeia*

I. H. GOLDBERGER, M. D.

Director of Health Education, New York City Public Schools

MARGUERITE P. DOLCH

GRACE T. HALLOCK

Director, Health and Welfare Publication Bureau
Metropolitan Life Insurance Company

ILLUSTRATIONS BY CORINNE MALVERN

GINN AND COMPANY

BOSTON · NEW YORK · CHICAGO · ATLANTA · DALLAS · COLUMBUS
SAN FRANCISCO · TORONTO · LONDON

GENESEE COUNTY LIBRARY

CONTENTS

Unit I · Your Habits

Off to the Woods, 1
You All Have Habits, 4
The Habit Game, 5
More Habits, 7
The Log Cabin, 9

Unit II · The First Thing in the Morning

The Next Morning, 15
Morning Habits, 17
How to Wash a Toothbrush, 19
A Place for Everything, 21
Getting Ready for Breakfast, 23
Start the Day Right, 24

Unit III · The Right Kinds of Food

Breakfast at the Log Cabin, 27
Mr. Jones's Store, 29
Fish for Dinner, 33
A Good Dinner, 34
Sunshine, Exercise, and Vitamins, 35
The Baby Gets Her Vitamins, 37
Milk Is the Best Food, 41
Keep Milk Clean and Cold, 42
Good-by to the Log Cabin, 43
Nancy's Story, 44

Unit IV · Dressing for Good Health

A Helper in the School Room, 47
Helpers in the Rain, 51
Helpers in the Winter, 54
Helpers in the Summer Time, 56
Help the Clothing Helpers, 58

Unit V · Cover Your Coughs and Sneezes

The Valentine Party, 63
Letters to Helen, 70
Why Miss Smith's Children Do Not Catch Colds, 74
Helen Writes a Letter, 75
Helen Has a Nurse, 76
Smallpox and Diphtheria, 78

Copyright, 1949, 1945, 1939, by Ginn and Company · Philippines Copyright, 1949, 1945, 1940, by Ginn and Company · All rights reserved
851.1

Unit VI · Nice Manners

Manners, 83
Please — Thank You — Excuse Me, 86
Little Sister Learns Habits, 87
Tom Shows How, 90
Getting Ready for Company, 92
Setting the Table, 96
When Company Comes, 99
At the Table, 100

Unit VII · The Five Doorways

A House with Five Doors, 103
The Eye Doorway, 104
First Aid for the Eyes, 108
The Ear Doorway, 110
First Aid for Billy's Ear, 111
The Nose Doorway, 114
First Aid for Nose Bleed, 115
The Mouth Doorway, 117
Do You Want These Things in Your Mouth? 118
Alcohol Harms, 119
The Skin Doorway, 120
At the Seashore, 121
Summer Care of the Skin, 123
Winter Care of the Skin, 123
The Story of Helen, 124

Unit VIII · Health and Sleep

Seven to Seven, 129
Sleeping and Growing, 133
Monkey Faces, 135
Going to Bed, 141

Unit IX · More Good Habits

Sport, 147
Walking Habits, 149
Sitting Habits, 151

Unit X · Always Be Careful

An Automobile on the Sidewalk, 157
Playing Is Lots of Fun, 167
The Safe Play Club, 168
The Meeting of the Safe Play Club, 170
Where to Play, 173
The White Box, 176
Jim's First Aid Kit, 178

VOCABULARY, 183

UNIT I

Your Habits

Off to the Woods

"Oh, what fun we are going to have!" said Nancy.

"Yes, we are," said Father. "We are going to live in a log cabin. We are going to live in the woods."

"Just smell this good fresh air!" said Dick.

"Out here the air smells so fresh and clean!" said Mother.

"Are you sure that you will like a log cabin?" asked Father.

"Oh, yes! Oh, yes!" said Nancy and Dick together.

"Living in the woods is not like living in the city," said Father.

"You can not do things here the way you are used to doing them at home in the city," said Mother.

"What things can't we do the same way?" asked Dick.

"You do many things every day without thinking about them," said Father. "You call them habits."

"Yes," said Nancy, "I know I have habits."

"You have the habit of turning on the light," said Father. "We shall have only a lamp at the cabin."

"I think a lamp will be fun," said Nancy. "I can learn to light it."

"You have the habit of turning on the water when you want a drink," said Father. "Now you will have to pump water."

"I like to pump water," said Dick. "It will be fun to learn new habits."

You All Have Habits

You all have habits. A habit is something you do without thinking about it.

You have been smiling at people you like from the time you were a baby. You smile at your friends. It is a habit. You do not think about it now.

You have many, many habits. You have habits in dressing. You have habits in eating. Do you have the habit of taking little bites?

You learn these habits. Then you do not think about them.

Something to Do

Make a list of good habits in eating. Do you have these habits?

The Habit Game

"Can't we play our Habit Game now?" asked Nancy.

"Why, yes," said Mother. "Let us play our Habit Game. When any one shows a good habit, say, 'Good Habit Helps.' When any one shows a bad habit, say, 'Bad Habit Harms.'"

"Every one in this bus has a good habit," laughed Father.

"All the people are sitting in their seats," said Dick.

"Good Habit Helps," said Nancy. "It is a good habit to sit in your seat when the bus goes."

"When I grow up," said Dick, "I am going to be a bus driver."

"A bus driver has to have good habits," said Father.

"Yes," said Dick. "I will always take care of my bus. I will keep my bus clean. I will look after the people that ride in my bus."

"Then I will ride with you," said Nancy.

"Good Habits always help," said Mother.

More Habits

The road began to turn. The bus driver slowed up.

"Good Habit Helps," said Father.

"Yes," said Mother. "The bus driver slows up when the road turns. That is a good habit."

"My!" said Dick, "I am hungry."

"Bad Habit Harms," said Nancy. "It is not good to eat between meals."

"We shall have our supper when we get to the cabin," said Mother.

Soon the bus stopped at a little store by the road.

"Here we are," said Father. "This is where we get off."

Nancy and Dick carefully got off the bus. Dick helped his mother off.

Father stopped to talk to the man at the store.

"Is everything ready for us at the cabin, Mr. Jones?"

"Yes," said Mr. Jones. "Just go up that little road, and you will see your cabin. It is the one with the screened porch."

They walked along the road. It went through the woods.

"There it is!" said Dick.

The little road had come to an end right by a log cabin with a big screened porch.

The Log Cabin

Dick went up to the door of the cabin.

"Oh," he laughed. "I was looking for the door bell."

Father laughed. "To use the door bell is a good habit when you call upon a friend. But we do not have a bell on a log cabin."

"Just open the door and walk in," said Mother.

Dick opened the door, and they went into a big room.

"We need fresh air," said Mother. She began to open the windows.

"Good Habit Helps," said Nancy, and helped to open the windows.

"Where is the dining room?" said Dick, looking all around.

"There is no dining room," said Father. "We shall use the porch for a dining room. Mother and I sleep in the living room. There is a bedroom where you and Nancy are to sleep."

"Well," said Nancy, "here is the kitchen. I know that because there is a stove in it."

"Good," said Mother. "Father will make a fire in the stove. We have brought our supper with us."

"My!" said Dick, "I am hungry." Nancy laughed.

"Dick is always hungry," she said.

"I will get you a good supper," said Mother.

"I think it's a little cold here," said Nancy. "Let us make a fire in the furnace."

"There is no furnace," said Father. "But Dick and I will go out and get some wood. We can make a fire in the stove and in the fireplace."

They had a good supper. They were hungry, and the food was so good! The fire in the fireplace was pretty. They sat in front of it and were warm and happy.

Things to Talk About

1. Here is a list of habits. Tell which habits are good. Tell which habits are bad. Tell why.

   a. Getting twelve hours of sleep every night.

   b. Drinking some glasses of water every day.

   c. Trading bites.

   d. Taking a bath with warm water and soap twice a week.

   e. Biting the bubble when you drink from the drinking fountain.

   f. Seeing your dentist twice a year.

   g. Drinking coffee.

   h. Eating between meals.

2. How many good habits do you have? Tell about some of them.

UNIT II

The First Thing in the Morning

The Next Morning

The next morning Nancy opened her eyes. She did not know where she was. She heard the birds singing. She heard the wind in the trees.

She looked across the room. There was Dick, just waking up. Both of them jumped out of bed at the same time and ran to the window. They stood and looked out.

"Good morning," said Mother. "But Dick, what do I see?"

Dick turned around.

"Oh, I forgot," he said. And he went to pick up some of his clothes from the floor.

"I did not see any hooks last night," he said.

"Hang clothes on a chair or on the foot of your bed, when there are no hooks," said Mother. "Never put them on the floor."

"Bad Habit Harms," said Nancy.

"It's time to dress, Dick," said Mother. "Take your clothes and dress in the living room. And hang up your night clothes when you are through."

So Dick went into the living room with his clothes.

Morning Habits

Father was sitting by the fireplace.

"I wish this place had a bathroom," said Dick.

Father laughed. "Most log cabins do not have bathrooms," he said. "Get dressed and go to the toilet. You must keep your good toilet habits to keep well."

Dick dressed. Then he went to the outdoor toilet in the woods back of the cabin.

When Dick got back he said, " Now I must wash my hands."

Dick took his washcloth and towel from hooks in the kitchen. Then he went to the washbasin outside the kitchen door.

Dick washed his face and hands. He washed his ears very carefully.

Then Dick got his toothbrush from its hook in the kitchen.

Dick brushed up and down, up and down. He brushed his front teeth. He brushed the teeth in the back of his mouth.

Dick brushed the inside of his teeth and the outside of his teeth. He knew just the right way to brush his teeth.

How to Wash a Toothbrush

Dick had to wash his toothbrush. At home he would have put it under the faucet. But there was no faucet in the cabin. There was just a bucket and a washbasin.

Of course he did not want to put a toothbrush into the bucket. Then he thought of what his father had told him the night before.

"In a cabin you must wash your toothbrush a new way. Take some water in a cup. Pour the water over the brush, then hang the brush up to dry."

"Hello, Dick," said Nancy. "I want to wash in the washbasin."

"It is fun getting dressed in a log cabin," said Dick. "We do the same things that we do in the city. But we do not do them in the same way."

Nancy got her own washcloth and towel off the hook. She washed in the washbasin.

Then she brushed her teeth and washed her toothbrush by pouring water over it.

"Now we have a new habit," said Nancy. "We must learn new habits in a log cabin."

A Place for Everything

Dick and Nancy went to their room. There was a mirror on the wall.

They took their combs. They looked in the mirror. They combed their hair. Then they set their combs side by side again under the mirror.

In the kitchen the toothbrushes were all hanging on hooks in a row, too. The towels and washcloths were in a row.

"Everything has a place," said Father. "Everything is in its place. That is a good habit."

Mother called: "Children, I need some helpers, please. We must put all the clothes away."

"Oh, yes, Mother," said Nancy. "We know. There must be a place for everything. Everything must be in its place."

"I am glad to hear you say that," said Mother. "When did you learn about that?"

"Father just told us," said Dick.

"Good," said Mother. "That is a fine habit."

Getting Ready for Breakfast

1. I hang up my night clothes.
2. I dress myself.
3. I wash my face and hands.
4. I brush my teeth.
5. I look in the looking glass.
6. I brush my hair.
7. I go to the toilet.
8. I wash my hands after going to the toilet.
9. And now I am ready for breakfast.

These are Dick and Nancy's Good Health Habits. How many of these Health Habits do you have?

Start the Day Right

You start the day right with good morning habits.

They help to *keep* you well. They help to make you *look* well. They help to make you *feel* well. They help to keep you *happy*.

Make a list of Dick and Nancy's Good Health Habits. Put this list on a card. Hang the card on the wall in your bathroom.

Look at the card every morning. See if you remember to do each thing on the list.

The Good Health Habits helped Dick and Nancy to have good health. They will help you to have good health, too.

What Have You Learned?

The words in the box finish sentences in the list. Find the right words to finish each sentence. What words in the box go with " They brush " ? The right words are " their teeth." Then 1 and g go together. The sentence says " They brush their teeth."

Do the same thing with the other words in the list. *Do not write in the book.*

a. their hands and faces	e. their clothes
b. their hair	f. the mirror
c. after going to the toilet	g. their teeth
d. their night clothes	h. the toilet

1. They brush _ _ ? _ _.
2. They put on _ _ ? _ _.
3. They look in _ _ ? _ _.
4. They wash _ _ ? _ _.
5. They go to _ _ ? _ _.
6. They comb _ _ ? _ _.
7. They wash their hands _ _ ? _ _.
8. They hang up _ _ ? _ _.

UNIT III

The Right Kinds of Food

Breakfast at the Log Cabin

"Hello, hello!" said Dick. "See what I have found. Blackberries! Blackberries for breakfast. I found them in the woods. See, I have a whole bucket full."

"My, they look good!" said Nancy. "I will wash the blackberries and put them in dishes."

"I helped to get this meal, too," said Father. "I got fresh milk and some butter from Mr. Jones at the store. I got some fresh eggs too."

"I made the whole-wheat toast," said Mother. "I made it over the fire in the kitchen stove. I cooked the eggs and the cereal."

"Who set the table out on the screened porch?" asked Father.

"I set the table," said Nancy. "I set it on the screened porch where no flies or bugs can get at our breakfast. I don't like to have flies and bugs eat with me."

A Good Breakfast

Blackberries		Brown cereal
Eggs	Butter	Milk
	Whole-wheat toast	

Mr. Jones's Store

"Good morning," said Mr. Jones. "What can I do for you this morning?"

"We have come for some food," said Nancy. "We know that good food helps to keep us well. Look, Mother, Mr. Jones has some oranges and bananas."

"Yes," said Mother, "fresh fruit is good for us. I will buy some oranges and bananas for dinner. And we want some brown cereal and some cocoa and whole-wheat bread."

"Mr. Jones, do you have any vitamins?" asked Nancy. "Our doctor told Mother to feed me vitamins."

Mr. Jones laughed.

"Of course I have vitamins," he said. "But you can not see them. They are in the food. The fruit and the brown cereal and the whole-wheat bread have vitamins in them."

"We want some fresh vegetables," said Mother. "Fresh vegetables are full of vitamins, too. That is why they help to keep us well."

Mr. Jones laughed again.

"Sunshine and exercise help you to keep well, too," he said. "And I can show you how you can have fresh vegetables and sunshine and exercise all together."

Mr. Jones took Nancy and her Mother out back of his store.

"Look at the fresh vegetables growing in the sunshine," he said. "Working in my garden gives me exercise too."

"Oh, Mother," said Nancy. "Could we have a garden?"

"Yes," said Mother. "We will have a garden. Then we can have fresh vegetables and exercise and sunshine all together."

"We will have vitamins too," laughed Nancy.

"I have everything in my store that you will need to make a garden," said Mr. Jones.

"May we buy some fresh vegetables from your garden now?" asked Mother.

"Yes," said Mr. Jones. "I can let you have fresh vegetables until your vegetables grow. You may have some spinach and a head of cabbage."

"Thank you, Mr. Jones, for letting us have some of your fresh vegetables," said Mother.

"Dick and I are going to have a garden by our cabin," said Nancy. "But we will come down and help you take care of your garden too."

"And I will tell you a story," said Mr. Jones. "I will tell you how to catch a fish four feet long."

Fish for Dinner

"See what we have!" cried Dick.

"Three big fish," said Nancy.

"Yes," said Father. "You should have seen Dick pull in that big one."

"It nearly jumped out of the boat," said Dick.

"If you will clean them," said Mother, "I will cook them for dinner."

"Fish for dinner," said Nancy. "Fish for dinner. We all like fish for dinner."

"We will all help Mother to get a good dinner," said Father.

A Good Dinner

Fish   Potatoes   Spinach
Raw-cabbage salad   Hot cocoa
Whole-wheat bread with butter
Bananas and oranges

Mother cooked a good dinner. They ate dinner on the screened porch, away from flies or bugs. Everybody was hungry. When hungry boys and girls have good food to eat, they grow big and strong.

Something to Do Together

Cut out pictures of foods to put on a table. Make a good dinner.

Cut out pictures of foods for a good breakfast.

Make a good supper in the same way.

Did you have any of these foods for your breakfast, dinner, or supper?

Sunshine, Exercise, and Vitamins

"Hello," said Mary. "I live in the white cabin on the big road."

"Hello," said Dick. "Come and see our garden."

"Do you like to work in your garden?" asked Mary.

"Oh, yes," said Nancy. "We like the sunshine and exercise."

"Look," said Dick. "We are going to have spinach for dinner. The spinach is out of our own garden."

"We have so much spinach," said Nancy. "You can have some, too."

"Thank you," said Mary. "My baby sister and I like spinach."

"Spinach is good for you. There are vitamins in spinach," said Dick.

Mary took the spinach that Dick gave her.

"Come over to our cabin and play with me," she said.

"I should like to come very much," said Nancy. "I will ask my mother."

"Ask your mother if you can come over to our cabin tomorrow," said Mary. "My baby sister is going to be one year old. Tomorrow we are going to have a birthday party."

The Baby Gets Her Vitamins

The next day Nancy went to see Mary. She saw Mary's little baby sister too. The baby was getting a sunbath.

"Oh, what a pretty baby!" said Nancy. "Does she like to take her sunbath?"

"Yes," said Mary. "But I have to be careful. I must not let her stay out in the sun too long. The sun will burn her skin and make it red. Sunburn makes your skin hurt."

"I like to take sunbaths, too," said Nancy. "Each day I stay in the sunshine just a little while. Then the sun makes my skin brown and healthy."

"Our doctor says that sunshine on our skin helps to make the sunshine vitamin," said Mary. "Sunshine helps to grow strong teeth and straight bones."

"Your baby sister is a big baby to be only a year old," said Nancy.

"She is big because Mother has given her the right kinds of food to eat," said Mary. "Our doctor told Mother just what food to give the baby."

"Milk is good for a baby," said Nancy. "Milk has vitamins in it. Vitamins help a baby to grow big and strong. Vitamins help to make straight bones."

"Yes," said Mary, "the doctor told us to give her other foods too. First she had orange juice, beef juice, and cod-liver oil. Then Mother gave her vegetables and eggs. She ate brown cereal too. Our baby has grown so big and strong. She can eat at the table with us."

"How much milk does she drink now?" asked Nancy.

"Our baby gets a quart of milk every day," said Mary. "And I drink a quart of milk every day, too."

"So do I," said Nancy.

Good Food
Milk

Orange juice		Beef juice
Cereal		Vegetables
Eggs	Cod-liver oil	Toast

Milk Is the Best Food

A quart of milk is four glasses of milk. Milk is one of the very best foods that boys and girls can have. Milk helps boys and girls to grow. There are many good things to eat that can be made with milk.

Hot soup is always good. Soup made with milk is the best kind. Milk soup is a good food for boys and girls.

Do you like puddings? Puddings made with milk are good. Most boys and girls like chocolate pudding.

Nancy likes to drink chocolate milk. Mary likes to drink cocoa.

They like to eat ice cream too. All foods that have milk in them are good for you.

Keep Milk Clean and Cold

"Mother, may I help you to clean the ice box?" asked Nancy.

"You are my good helper," said Mother. "You clean the ice box. Then I can get the vegetables ready for dinner."

"The ice box must be very clean," said Nancy.

"Yes," said Mother. "Milk must be kept clean and cold in the ice box. Meat and butter must be kept cold, too. And green vegetables keep fresh longer if they are kept cold."

Good-by to the Log Cabin

No one wanted to go back to the city.

"I like to play outdoors in the woods," said Dick.

"I like to use a lamp," said Nancy. "And I like to watch the fire in the fireplace."

"A pump is fun," said Dick.

"But a faucet is nice," said Father.

"When it gets cold we shall be glad to have a furnace," said Mother. "We can come to the cabin again next year."

So the Browns got ready to go back to the city. They said good-by to the cabin in the woods. They said good-by to Mr. Jones at the store. They got on the bus and went back to the city.

Nancy's Story

Nancy is in the second grade. She wrote a story about good foods to eat. And this is what she wrote.

"Good Foods to Eat are Foods that are Good for You."

Miss Smith, her teacher, thought that was a good story. She asked Nancy to tell the second grade " What foods are good for you."

So Nancy told about Mary's baby sister. She told about the baby's food that helped her to grow.

" Nancy has given us some things to think about," said Miss Smith. " Let me write them down. We all want to know what foods to eat to help us to grow big and strong and to be healthy.

Stop and Think
Do You Do These Things?

1. Do you take cod-liver oil? It has vitamins in it that help to make your teeth and bones strong.

2. Do you drink orange juice or tomato juice? It helps to keep you well.

3. Do you eat carrots and string beans? Do you eat lettuce and spinach? All vegetables are good for you.

4. Do you eat apples, bananas, and other fruits? They are good for you.

5. Do you eat eggs and meat? Eggs and meat will help to make you grow big and strong.

6. Do you eat cereals? A hot cereal is good for breakfast.

7. Do you drink four cups of milk each day? Milk is the best food of all.

Remember. Good foods to eat are foods that are good for you.

UNIT IV

Dressing for Good Health

A Helper in the School Room

"I have a helper in this room that I want you to know," said Miss Smith.

The children of the second grade looked all around the room.

"My helper has a little red tongue," said Miss Smith. "Sometimes his tongue is long. Sometimes it is short."

"Oh, Miss Smith," said Alice, "my tongue does not get long when I talk. It does not get short. It stays right inside my mouth."

Miss Smith laughed. "My helper is not a little girl," she said. "My helper is not a little boy. My helper tells me how warm the school room is. Look! there he is upon the wall."

"A thermometer! A thermometer!" cried the children.

"Yes, that is right," said Miss Smith. "When the room is very warm, the thermometer's red tongue gets long. And when the room gets colder, his red tongue gets short."

"The thermometer talks with its red tongue," laughed Alice.

"We work best indoors," said Miss Smith, "when the thermometer's red tongue is at 68. If it goes down to 64, we feel cold. If the red tongue goes above 72, we feel so warm that we get tired and sleepy."

Miss Smith looked at the thermometer on the wall. The red tongue said 74.

"What can we do?" asked Miss Smith.

"We can open a window," said Jane.

"We can open a window from the bottom to let the fresh air in," said Tom.

"We can open the window from the top to let the hot air out," said Sam.

So Miss Smith opened the window from the top. She opened the window from the bottom too.

All the children stood up and took exercises.

"Now it is not too hot," said Miss Smith. "The thermometer says 68. We can get back to work."

"Let us watch our thermometer every day," said Jerry. "We do not want the room to get too warm."

"Good," said Miss Smith. "Let us watch our school-room helper every day."

Helpers in the Rain

"What are some helpers that can keep you from getting wet?" asked Miss Smith.

"Rubbers," said Mary.

"A raincoat," said Jerry.

"An umbrella," said Tom.

"When it looks like rain," said Miss Smith, "always remember your helpers. Your rubbers, raincoats, and umbrellas are good helpers."

"Once I went out to play and it rained," said Jack. "I got wet and cold, and then I was sick."

"If you had put on dry clothes right away, you might not have been sick," said Miss Smith. "Wet clothes make your skin cold. Then you may get sick."

"Mother makes me change my clothes if I get wet," said Jerry.

"My mother told me something, too," said Nancy. "Hold up an umbrella so that you can see when you cross a street."

"You must look to see if an automobile is coming," said Sue.

"And do not point the umbrella at some one's face," said Dave.

"My boys and girls have good safety habits," said Miss Smith. "And they have good health habits too."

Helpers in the Winter

"Have you heard this poem?" asked Miss Smith.

> The North Wind will blow,
> And we shall have snow,
> And what will poor Robin do then?
> > Poor thing!

> He will sit in a barn
> To keep himself warm,
> And hide his head under his wing.
> > Poor thing!

"Poor Robin is cold when the North Wind blows," said Mary.

"Well," said Jerry, "I like the poem. But when the North Wind blows I am not a 'poor thing.'"

"Do you sit in the house and keep yourself warm?" asked Miss Smith.

"No," said Jerry. "I put on a warm coat and hat and overshoes. Then I go out and play in the snow."

"The warm clothes help to keep your body warm," said Miss Smith. "They help to keep the heat of your body inside you. When it is cold outdoors, remember your helpers."

Helpers in the Summer Time

"Should you like to wear a big warm coat in the summer time?" asked Miss Smith.

"No," said Tom. "It would make me too hot."

"Warm clothes keep the heat from leaving your body," said Miss Smith. "That is why they make you feel hot."

"In the summer I wear a play suit," said Alice. "It is cooler."

"Sometimes I wear a swimming suit," said Jerry.

"I do not wear very many clothes in the summer," said Tom. "Now I know why I feel so much cooler in a sun suit."

"In the summer we want to keep cool," said Miss Smith. "In winter we want to keep warm by keeping in the heat that our bodies make. We do not want our bodies to be too hot or too cold. We want them to be just warm enough."

Help the Clothing Helpers

They Want to Help You

I am a nice red raincoat. One rainy day Mary left me hanging up at home. I could not help Mary. She got wet going to school. Please remember me when it rains.

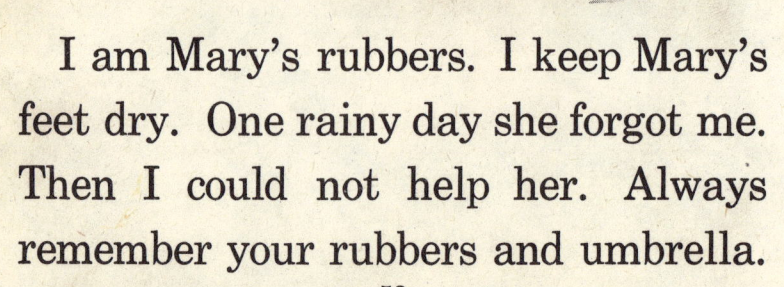

I am Mary's rubbers. I keep Mary's feet dry. One rainy day she forgot me. Then I could not help her. Always remember your rubbers and umbrella.

I am Tom's warm winter coat. I keep him warm on cold days. He always takes me off when he goes into school.

I am Tom's warm overshoes. When it snows, I keep Tom's feet warm and dry. When the snow is on the ground or when it rains, Tom puts me on.

One day Tom did not take me off when he went into the school room. I made Tom's feet too hot. Tom did not feel well. Please remember to take off your overshoes when you are indoors.

I am Alice's red snow suit. I am her clothing helper in the winter time. I keep her dry and warm.

I am a pretty blue sweater. Alice likes to wear me very much. One day Alice forgot to take me off when she went into the school room. I made her too hot. When she went out to play she caught cold. Please remember to take your sweater off when you go into a warm room. Your sweater will make you too hot indoors.

What Have You Learned?

Find the right end for each sentence:

1. In winter we work best in school when the thermometer is at __?__.

> 98   68   64   72

2. If the thermometer goes above 72, we feel __?__.

> tired and sleepy   cold   sick

3. Rubbers, raincoats, and umbrellas are our clothing helpers in __?__.

> winter   summer   rain

4. Warm coats and overshoes are our clothing helpers in __?__.

> winter   summer   rain

5. In winter we wear clothes to keep in the __?__.

> heat   cold   rain

6. In summer we want to keep __?__.

> cool   hot   wet

UNIT V

Cover Your Coughs and Sneezes

The Valentine Party

The children of the second grade were going to have a Valentine Party. They were going to ask their mothers to come to the Valentine Party.

The children were making big red hearts. They were going to string the hearts and hang them up.

They were not telling their mothers how pretty they were making their room. It was a secret. They were going to surprise their mothers.

"I like secrets," said Alice.

Billy was making a big heart, and Alice was helping him.

"Kerchoo! Kerchoo!" sneezed Billy.

"Oh, Billy," said Alice, "when you want to cough or sneeze you should cover your mouth and nose with your handkerchief. Don't you know that?"

"Kerchoo! Kerchoo! Kerchoo!" sneezed Billy. "I can't find my handkerchief."

"Oh, Billy," said Alice, "now maybe I shall sneeze, too. If you do not cover up your sneeze, you may give one of us your cold."

Just then Tom sneezed, "Kerchoo! Kerchoo!" He tried to cover up his sneeze with his hand.

"Are we going to have colds and sneezes for our Valentine Party?" asked Miss Smith. "That would be too bad. I do not want any boy or girl to miss the Valentine Party."

"Please may I wash my hands, Miss Smith?" asked Tom. "I had to cover my sneeze with my hand."

"Yes, go and wash your hands, Tom," said Miss Smith. "Cold germs are on your hand. And I will give you a paper handkerchief to cover up your coughs and sneezes. Some of you forgot your handkerchiefs today. If you have a cold, you must have a handkerchief. Carry one in your pocket all the time."

"May I have a paper handkerchief, too, please?" asked Billy. "I feel another sneeze coming."

"Kerchoo! Kerchoo!" sneezed Nancy. She found her handkerchief in time to put it over her mouth and nose.

Miss Smith got out a box of paper handkerchiefs.

"Any one who forgot a handkerchief may come and get one of these," she said. "A paper handkerchief will catch the germs. But tell me why so many of my boys and girls are sneezing today. What has happened to you? What did you do yesterday?"

"I went to Jimmy's birthday party," said Billy.

"So did I," said Nancy.

"And I did, too," said Tom.

"Oh," said Miss Smith. "Was there some one at Jimmy's birthday party yesterday who had a cold?"

"Helen is not at school today," said Alice. "But she was at the party yesterday."

"Yes," said Nancy. "And she sneezed right in my face when we were playing whispering secrets."

"How do you play whispering secrets?" asked Miss Smith.

"You sit in a circle," said Billy.

"And you whisper the secret to the one next to you in the circle," said Nancy.

"But the secret gets changed going around the circle," said Alice. "The last one has to tell what he heard. And then the first one tells what the secret was when it started. It's fun."

"Well," said Miss Smith. "I think that I know the secret of the sneezes. Helen brought her cold to Jimmy's birthday party. When she sneezed into the air, she gave her cold to the boys and girls who were near her."

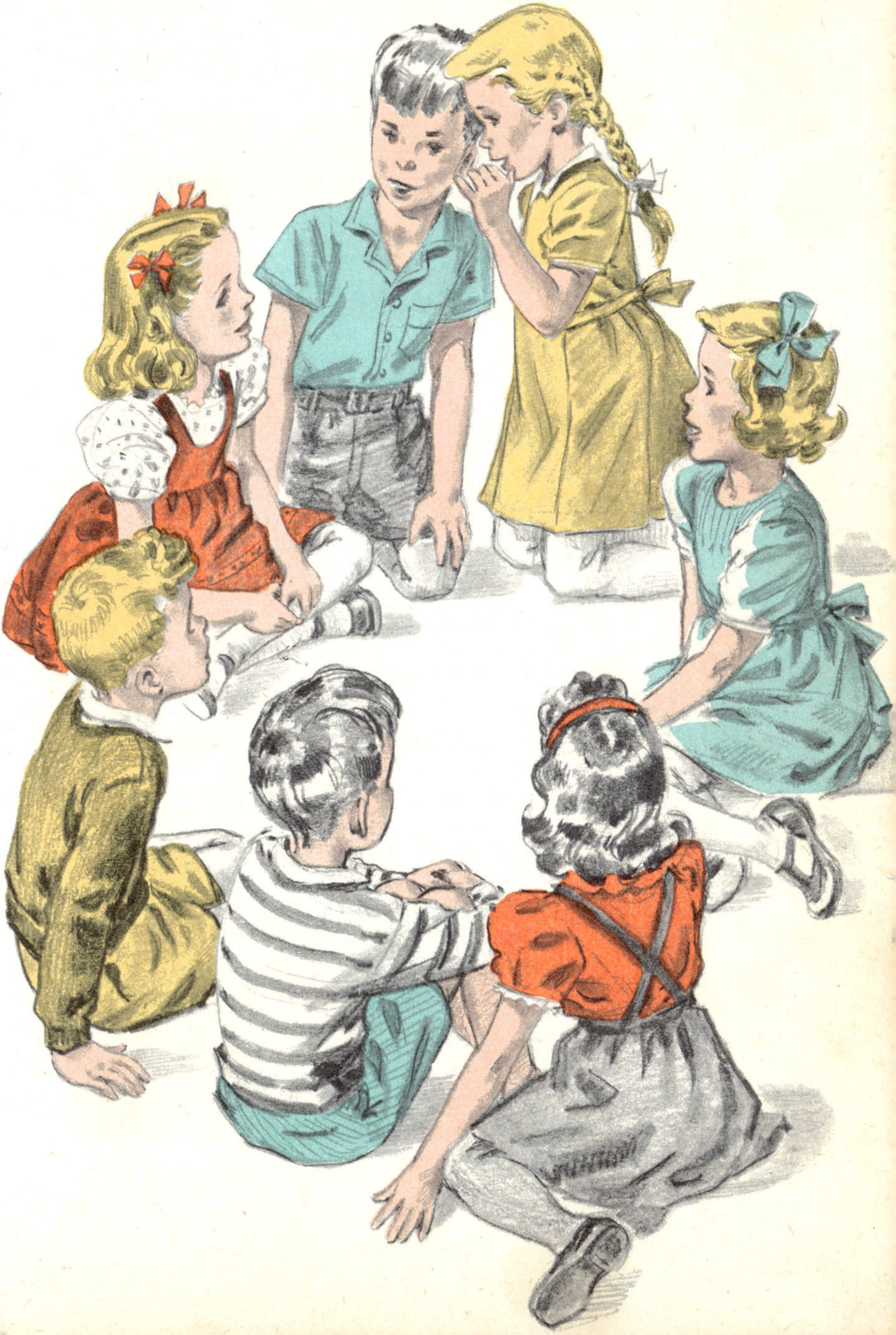

Letters to Helen

"Let us write letters to Helen," said Tom.

"Let us tell her that we want her to come back to school," said Betty.

"Let us ask her to be careful with her sneezes," said Alice.

"Let us tell her what we have learned about colds," said Dave.

Here are some of the letters that they wrote to Helen.

Jane's Letter

Dear Helen,

I am sorry you have a cold. Of course you must have got your cold from some one who had a cold. Colds are catching.

Miss Smith is telling us about good health habits. She does not want us to catch cold.

Please get well soon.

                    Your friend,
                        Jane

Billy's Letter

Dear Helen,

We learned something new today.

Miss Smith said: "Germs give us colds. Germs get into the air when you cough or sneeze."

Every one should cover up a sneeze or a cough with a handkerchief. Then your cold germs will not get into the air.

We all want you to get well soon.

                    Your friend,
                        Billy

Tom's Letter

Dear Helen,

Mother asked the doctor what to do to keep me from catching cold.

Here are some of the things he said:

Eat vitamin foods. Vitamins help you to grow and to be strong.

Take cod-liver oil. It has vitamins in it, too.

Drink some water every day.

Play in the sunshine.

Sleep twelve hours every night.

Keep strong and healthy.

I am going to do these things.

I do not think that I am going to have a cold.

                Your friend,
                Tom

Why Miss Smith's Children Do Not Catch Colds

Billy says, "I keep away from any one with a cold."

Nancy says, "I do not put my fingers in my mouth."

Tom says, "I wash my hands before I eat."

Alice says, "I drink four glasses of milk every day."

Dave says, "I eat good health foods."

Mary says, "I take cod-liver oil."

Jimmy says, "I like a room when the thermometer says 68."

Jane says, "I sleep twelve hours each night with my window open."

Miss Smith says: "The children cover their sneezes and coughs. They do not give colds to others."

Helen Writes a Letter

Helen was in bed. She was glad to get the letters from her friends. She wrote a letter to them.

Dear Boys and Girls,

Thank you for your letters. I am sorry I nearly gave you my cold.

The doctor said I must stay in bed. That will help me to get over my cold very quickly. I have a very good nurse.

I want to come to the Valentine Party. I have learned many things about colds from your letters.

      Your friend,
      Helen

Miss Smith read Helen's letter to the second grade.

Helen Has a Nurse

Helen came back to school in time for the Valentine Party.

"Tell us about your nurse," asked Nancy.

Helen laughed. "My nurse had a clean white apron. She put the apron on over her dress.

"It was your mother with an apron on," said Nancy.

"Yes," said Helen. "I learned some good health habits from my nurse."

Don't Blow Your Nose Hard

Some of the cold germs might go into your ear and make it hurt.

Use Paper Handkerchiefs

Put a paper bag at the side of the bed. Put the used paper handkerchiefs into the bag. Then burn the bag.

"If you do get a cold," said Miss Smith, "do as Helen did. You should stay in bed until you are well. Some of the good health habits will help you to get well, too. You should eat the right things. You should take cod-liver oil. You should drink fruit juices. You should drink plenty of water."

Smallpox and Diphtheria

"Years ago," said Miss Smith, "many children had smallpox. And many children had diphtheria. The children were very sick.

"It was often a long, long time before they were strong and healthy children again.

"Years ago doctors did not know how to keep children from getting smallpox or diphtheria.

"But now doctors know how to vaccinate you against smallpox. Then you will never get smallpox. They can give you injections to make you safe from diphtheria.

"All boys and girls should be vaccinated against smallpox. All boys and girls should have injections to make them safe from diphtheria."

Have you been vaccinated against smallpox?

Have you had injections to make you safe from diphtheria?

What Have You Learned?

Find the words in the box that finish each sentence in the list. What words in the box go with " Milk is a _ _ ? _ _ "? The right words are "*f.* good health food." Do the same thing with the other words in the box. *Do not write in the book.*

---

a. from any one with a cold   *f.* good health food
b. in the winter time   *g.* each day
c. water every day   *h.* each night
d. coughs and sneezes   *i.* is good for you
e. when you have a cold

---

1. Milk is a _ _ ? _ _.
2. Cover your _ _ ? _ _.
3. Play in the sunshine _ _ ? _ _.
4. Keep away _ _ ? _ _.
5. Wear warm clothes _ _ ? _ _.
6. Drink plenty of _ _ ? _ _.
7. Cod-liver oil _ _ ? _ _.
8. Sleep twelve hours _ _ ? _ _.
9. Stay in bed _ _ ? _ _.

Stop and Think

Do You Do These Things?

1. Rest a little each day?

2. Sleep twelve hours each night with the window open?

3. Eat good health foods?

Milk	Lettuce	Raw carrots
Eggs	Spinach	Tomatoes
Meat	Raw cabbage	Brown cereals

Whole-wheat bread and butter

4. Take cod-liver oil?

5. Drink plenty of orange juice?

6. Drink plenty of water every day?

7. Play in the sunshine?

8. Keep away from any one who has a cold?

UNIT VI

Nice Manners

Manners

"Did you have a good time at the Valentine Party?" asked Miss Smith.

"Oh, yes, yes!" said the boys and girls of the second grade.

"My mother had a good time, too," said Alice. "She thought the boys and girls had very nice manners."

"What are manners?" asked Jimmy.

"Manners are the way you do things," said Alice.

"Jimmy, I think that you have good manners." Jimmy looked surprised.

"Yes," said Miss Smith. "At the Valentine Party I saw you get up and give your chair to Mrs. Brown."

Jimmy smiled and said, "Mrs. Brown said, 'Thank you, Jimmy.'"

"'Thank you' is a nice thing to say," said Miss Smith.

"I heard Tom say 'please' when he asked Mary to open the door," said Alice.

"I always try to remember not to walk in front of any one," said Ruth.

"I say 'Excuse me' if I have to go in front of people," said Tom.

"If you always try to have good manners," said Miss Smith, "pretty soon you will do nice things without thinking about it."

"Good manners will be habits then," said Alice.

"That is right," said Miss Smith. "Every one had a good time at our Valentine Party because you boys and girls had good manners. They were your good habits of being nice to other people."

Things to Talk About

Tell about some good manners you have when you eat, when you have a cold.

How do you show good manners when you come to a party?

How do you show good manners when you go home from a party?

Please — Thank You — Excuse Me

Please, thank you, and excuse me
Are the nicest words to say
To Mother and to Father
For what they do each day.

Please, may I have a glass of milk?
Thank you, then I'll say.
And now excuse me, Mother, dear,
It's time to go and play.

Please, thank you, and excuse me
Are the nicest words to say.
Try them once, try them twice,
You will like to talk that way.

Little Sister Learns Habits

Tommy's little sister was learning to eat all by herself. She sat up in a high chair at the table. She had a little knife and fork and spoon. But she had to learn how to use them.

"Tom," said Mother, "we shall have to teach Little Sister the right way to eat. We want her to have nice table manners."

"May I be her teacher?" asked Tom.

"Yes," said Mother. "I think that you will make a good teacher. What shall you do first?"

"First," said Tom, "I shall have to teach her to take little bites. She takes too much food on her spoon. And then she tries to put it all into her mouth at once."

So Tom showed her how to take only a little food on her spoon.

"Oh, Mother," said Tom. "I have just made up a little poem for sister."

> Little bites and chew,
> Little bites and chew,
> That's what you're to do,
> That's what you're to do.

Baby Sister laughed and laughed.

Baby Sister tried very hard to do just as Tom had told her to do.

"That is fine," said Tom. "But chew each bite and chew it slowly. Chew with your mouth closed, too."

Baby Sister shut her mouth. She chewed and chewed.

"That looks much better," said Tom.

"You're a good teacher, Tom," said Mother. "And Little Sister learns good habits very quickly."

Tom Shows How

The next day Tom tried to show Baby Sister how to use a knife and fork.

"See," said Tom, "first you sit up straight and tall. Then you take the fork in your left hand. You take your knife in your right hand. Now you put the fork on the meat to hold it still. Then you cut the meat into little pieces with the knife."

Baby Sister watched Tom carefully.

"After you have cut the meat," Tom said, "you must take the fork in your right hand. Use the fork to put the little piece of meat into your mouth."

Baby Sister watched Tom. He put a piece of meat on her plate. With her fork she put the piece of meat into her mouth.

"Oh, Mother," said Tom, "I think Baby Sister is too little to cut her meat. But she can use the fork in her right hand to put the little piece of meat into her mouth. Soon she will have nice table manners."

"Pretty soon," said Mother, "Baby Sister will have the right habits of eating."

Getting Ready for Company

Ruth and Peter had just come home from school. They were hungry. They went into the kitchen to get some food to eat. Mother gave them a glass of milk and some whole-wheat bread and butter.

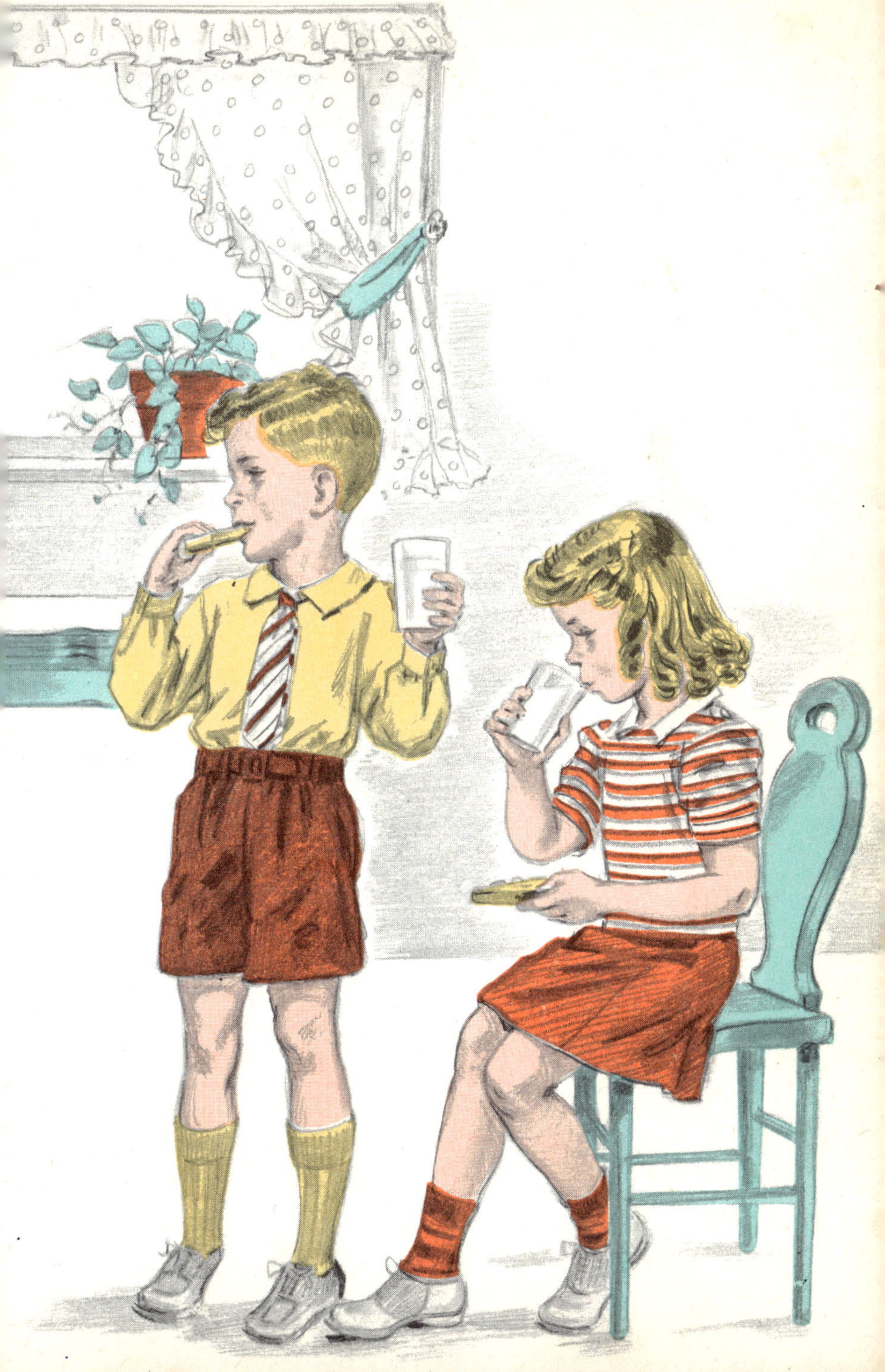

"Mr. Jones is coming for dinner tonight," said Mother.

"Good," said Ruth. "May I help put on the long tablecloth?"

"May I put on the knives and forks?" said Peter.

"Yes," said Mother.

Ruth and Peter went to the washroom to wash their hands. They remembered that Miss Smith had told them, "Germs do not like clean hands."

"We must have clean hands when we put on the tablecloth," said Ruth.

"We must have clean hands when we put on the knives and forks, too," said Peter.

So the children helped to set the table.

"What are we going to have for dinner tonight?" asked Peter.

"Can't you smell the roast beef cooking?" asked Mother.

"It makes me hungry," said Ruth.

"I got some fresh tomatoes, green beans, and celery," said Mother. "We shall have the inside pieces of the celery on the salad."

"Your dinners are always good, Mother," said Ruth.

This is what the family were going to have for dinner.

	Fruit cup	
Roast beef		Potatoes
Green beans	Tomato and lettuce salad	
	Celery	
	Whole-wheat rolls and butter	
Milk		Water
Ice cream		Chocolate cake

Setting the Table

Before long the company table was set. The tablecloth was snowy white. The napkins at each place were snowy white, too.

Ruth knew just where to put the knives and forks. At each place she put the knife at the right of the plate. She put the glass above it. She put the fork at the left of the plate. She put the napkin at the left, too.

Peter remembered that there was to be a salad for dinner. So he put a salad fork at the side of the first fork.

Ruth remembered that the first thing they were going to have for dinner was a fruit cup. So she put on a spoon next to the knife.

"A pretty table always helps us to enjoy dinner more," said Mother. " Now, if you children have finished setting the table, go and get cleaned up for dinner. We will pour the water the last thing so that it will be cold."

Peter and Ruth went up to their rooms.

" I'll get dressed first," said Peter to Ruth.

" I'll be first," said Ruth to Peter.

Ruth washed while Peter shined his shoes. Then Peter washed just as clean as he knew how.

As fast as they could, they put on clean clothes. Ruth put on her best dress.

Then they heard Father at the door.

When Company Comes

Father came into the house with Mr. Jones.

"Hello, hello, everybody!" Father called. "I want Mr. Jones to meet my family."

Peter and Mother and Ruth went to meet Mr. Jones. He was a nice, big, friendly man.

"Mr. Jones," said Father, "I want you to meet my family. This is Mrs. White, and Ruth, and Peter."

"I am glad to meet you," said Mr. Jones. "I am happy to come and have dinner with you tonight. I always enjoy a family dinner."

"And we are very glad that you could come," said Mother.

The White family made Mr. Jones feel very much at home.

At the Table

Ruth and Peter liked to be at the table with company. They sat up straight. They used their napkins carefully. They finished chewing food before they took a drink of water. They ate everything that was put on their plates.

Mr. Jones talked with Ruth and Peter. He asked Ruth how she liked her school. He asked Peter if he had a dog.

The children liked to talk to him. But they did not talk too much. They did not talk with food in their mouths. They were still while Mr. Jones and Mother and Father talked. They all enjoyed the good company dinner.

Stop and Think
Do You Do These Things?

1. Do you make company feel at home?

2. Do you take little bites of food?

3. Do you eat slowly?

4. Do you chew with your mouth closed?

5. Do you sit up straight and tall at the table?

6. Do you eat everything on your plate?

UNIT VII

The Five Doorways

A House with Five Doors

"I am going to tell you about a house with five doors," said Miss Smith.

"It must be a very big house," said Alice. "Our house has only a front door and a back door. Why should any house need five doors?"

Miss Smith laughed.

"Five things want to get into this house," she said. "And there is a door for each one."

"What a funny house!" said Alice.

The Eye Doorway

Your eyes are the doorway for everything you see.

You can read the stories in this book with your eyes.

But you must have good light when you read. If the sun is on your book, there will be too much light. It will hurt your eyes.

If you read when it is too dark, your eyes will hurt.

In school, be sure you have a good light on your book.

At home, be sure you have a good light on your book.

The light should not shine into your eyes. The light should be behind you or above you. It should come from the right or the left side.

Always read in a good light.

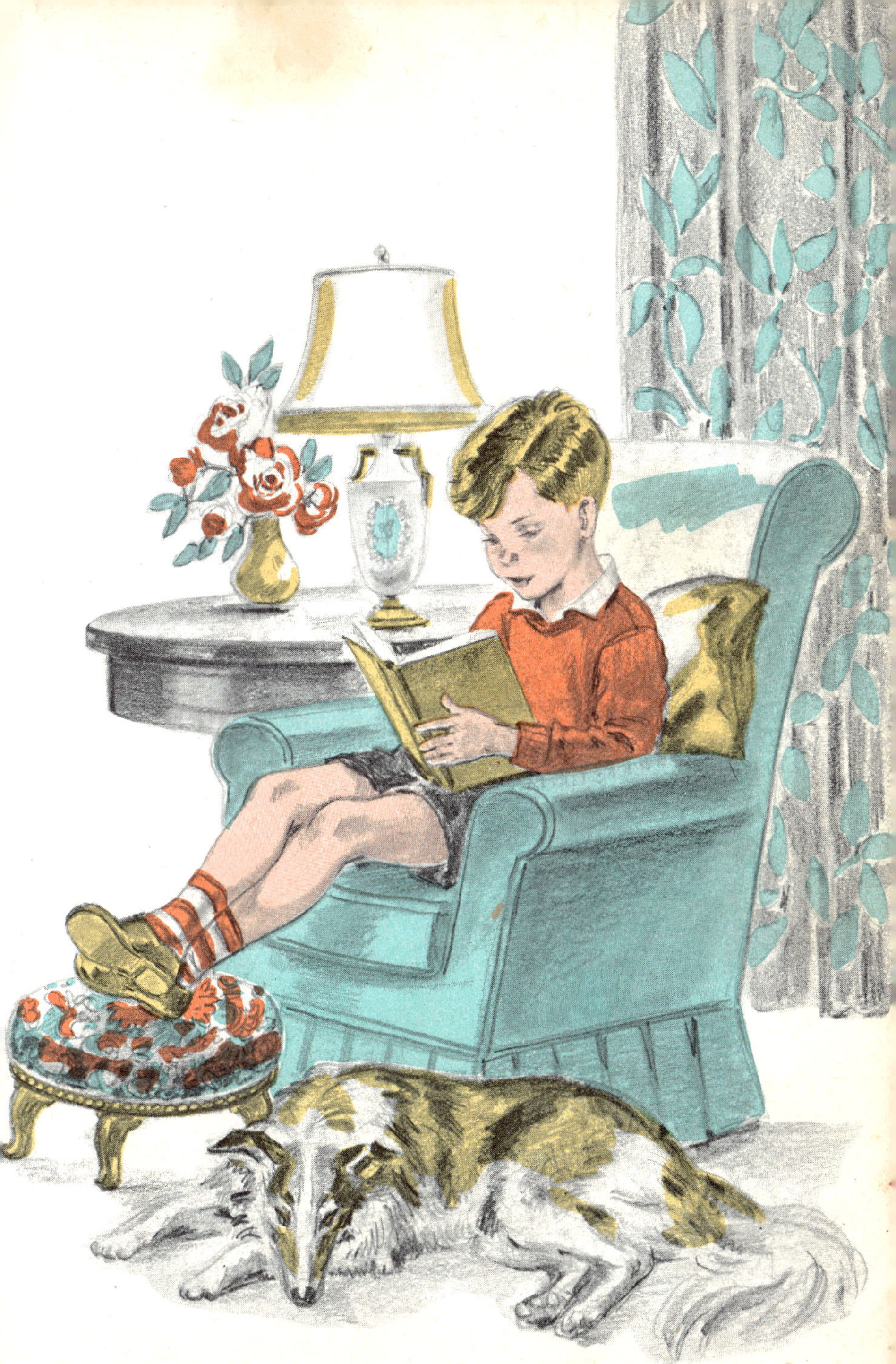

When you read, sit so that you hold the book just right. Do not hold your book too close to your eyes. Do not hold your book too far away from your eyes. Ask your teacher to watch you when you read. She can tell if you are holding your book just right.

When you read, sit straight and tall. Then you will not get tired while you read.

Always be careful of your eyes when you read.

Always read in a good light.

Things to Talk About

1. Is there good light in your school room? Does it come from your right or left side?

2. Do you have good light to read by at home? Do you sit so that the reading lamp is behind you and on your right or left side?

3. How close to your eyes should you hold the book when you read? Ask your teacher.

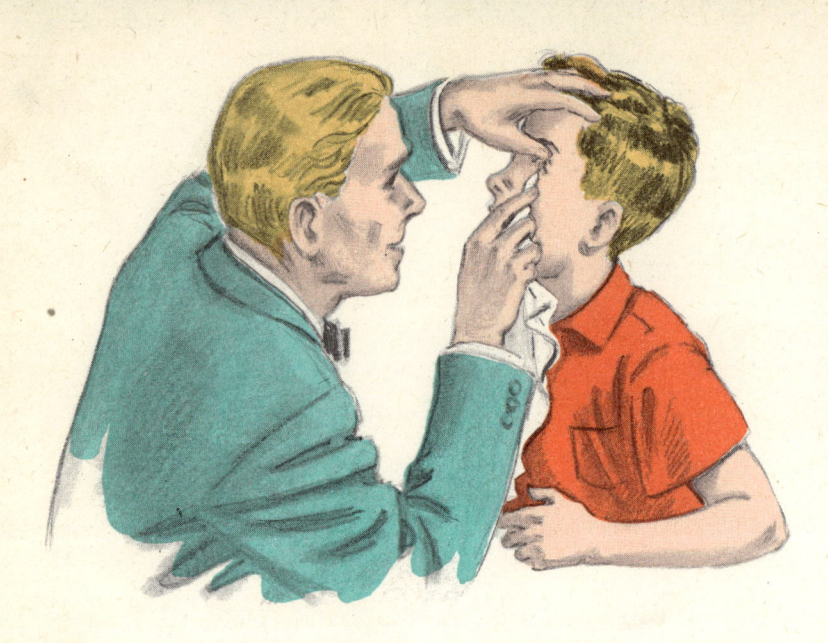

First Aid for the Eyes

If a little piece of dirt should get into your eyes, do not rub your eyes. Go at once to some one who can help you to get it out.

The water, or tears, in your eye will help to wash the little piece of dirt out. The tears help to keep your eye clean. But if you should rub your eyes, the dirt might cut and hurt your eye.

Dirty hands may rub more dirt into your eyes. Use a clean handkerchief to get something out of your eye.

When you wash your face, use a clean washcloth. A dirty washcloth may get germs into your eyes.

Some boys and girls have to wear glasses to help their eyes to see. If the doctor tells you to wear glasses when you read, be sure to do so.

If you wear glasses when you play, be careful not to break them. Keep your glasses clean, so that your eyes can see through them.

When you play, be careful of your eyes. And be careful of the eyes of the children you are playing with. Do not throw sand. It might get into children's eyes.

Always be careful of your eyes.

The Ear Doorway

The ears are the doorway for everything you hear. Do you like to hear beautiful music? Do you like to hear the music the birds make? Do you like to hear your mother read? There are other beautiful sounds you like to hear.

Be very careful not to let anything hurt your ears. Keep them clean. Do not put anything hard into them. Keep your fingers out of your ears. The sharp point of anything might hurt the little place inside your ear that you hear with.

Never hit any one on the ear. To hit the ear may hurt it badly.

Here is a story about something that happened to one boy's ear.

First Aid for Billy's Ear

Billy was so happy! He was going to camp for a whole week.

Father put him into a car with some other boys. They were all going to camp.

"Good-by, Father," said Billy. "I shall not see you for a whole week."

"Good-by, Billy," said Father. "Have a good time. Be careful not to get hurt."

When they first got to camp Billy had a fine time. He helped the other boys to get wood for a big bonfire. A bonfire is lots of fun.

But something happened to Billy. A little bug got into his ear. Without thinking, Billy put his finger into his ear. Now the little bug was 'way back inside of Billy's ear.

"Oh! Oh! Oh!" cried Billy. "Something is in my ear."

But no one could see anything in Billy's ear, because the bug had gone 'way inside.

"Oh! Oh! Oh!" cried Billy. "It hurts."

One of the big boys took Billy home to his father in an automobile. His father took Billy at once to a doctor.

"Now, Billy," said the doctor, "what happened?"

Then Billy told him about the little bug. The doctor got some warm oil and put it into Billy's ear. The little bug that was 'way inside of Billy's ear was washed out by the warm oil.

"Next time that anything gets into your ear, Billy," said the doctor, "do not put your finger in your ear. Go at once to some one who can help you to get it out."

The Nose Doorway

Your nose is a doorway for good fresh air. You must have fresh air to live. Your nose warms up the air before it goes inside you.

Do you like to smell roast beef cooking? The smell of good food makes you hungry. You smell through your nose.

You do not want to hurt your nose. Never put things into your nose. Never put your fingers into your nose. That is not a clean habit. You might hurt the inside of your nose. Do not hit any one on the nose. The nose may start to bleed.

Take good care of your nose doorway.

First Aid for Nose Bleed

Dave had been playing too hard at recess time. He was running so fast that he did not look where he was going.

Dave had a bad fall and hit his nose. It started to bleed. And so he ran to Miss Smith. He knew that Miss Smith would give him first aid for nose bleed.

Miss Smith put a clean handkerchief in cold water.

"Hold your head up, Dave," she said.

"Put this cold handkerchief on your nose. It will help to stop the bleeding."

"That feels good," said Dave. "Only one side of my nose is bleeding now."

Miss Smith gave Dave a paper handkerchief.

"Hold this against the side of your nose that is bleeding," said Miss Smith. "It will help to stop the bleeding."

"Thank you, Miss Smith," said Dave. "The bleeding has stopped. Next time I will be more careful."

"Be careful not to hit your nose again," said Miss Smith.

The Mouth Doorway

The mouth is another doorway. Good things to eat and good things to drink go into your mouth. Put only good clean things into this doorway.

In your mouth are your nice white teeth. Good strong teeth help you to chew your food. Drink milk and take cod-liver oil every day to help make them strong.

Do not eat too much candy. Candy may hurt your teeth. Wash out your mouth with water after eating candy.

Brush your teeth after you eat to keep them clean. Clean teeth look nice and feel nice.

Never run with anything in your mouth. If you fell, it might hurt your mouth. Do not try to bite hard things. You might break your teeth.

Do You Want These Things in Your Mouth?

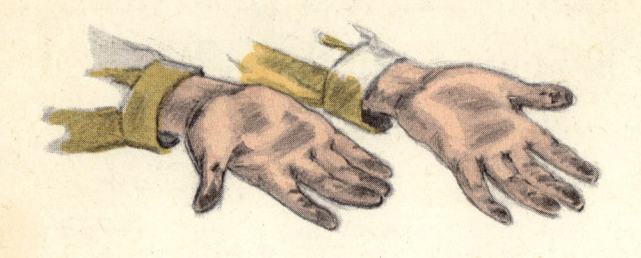

Do you put dirty fingers into your mouth?

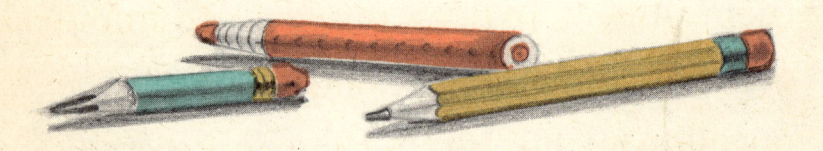

Pencils may have dirt on them.
Keep your fingers out of your mouth. Do not put your pencil into your mouth. It might have germs on it. Keep your mouth clean.

Take care of the mouth doorway. Keep it clean. Eat and drink only good clean food.

Alcohol Harms

Drinks that have alcohol in them are not good for any one to drink. Alcohol is not a food. It does not do you any good. You do not want to put into the mouth doorway anything that harms you.

Alcohol harms. It does not help you to grow. It does not help to make you strong. It does not help to make you healthy. Every one wants to be strong and healthy. Buy only drinks that are good for you.

Milk is the best drink of all. It helps you to grow. It helps to make you healthy. Fruit juices are good for you. They have vitamins in them. And vitamins help to keep you strong and healthy.

The Skin Doorway

The skin is a doorway, too. Feeling comes to you through your skin. The skin on your fingers helps you to learn about things by touching them.

Your skin tells you how warm it is. It tells you how cold it is. If it is cold, you can put on a warm coat. Then when you go out to play you will not feel cold.

You should keep your skin clean. Wash your hands and face often. Take a bath twice a week.

You must be very careful if you have a cut on your skin. Be sure to wash all the dirt out of the cut. Use soap and warm water. Germs are in the dirt. You do not want germs to get inside you. If the cut is very bad, go to a doctor.

At the Seashore

Dave and his mother were going to the seashore. It was the first time they had gone to the seashore. They had their lunch in a basket.

"I can play all day," said Dave. "I can play all day long in the sun."

Soon they got to the seashore. Mother got a big umbrella and a chair. She sat under the umbrella and watched Dave play.

Dave ran on the sand. He played with other children. They made a big sand house.

"Dave," called his mother. "Do you want to sit under the umbrella?"

"Oh," laughed Dave, "I do not want to sit under the umbrella. Let me play in the sand until lunch time."

"You should not stay out in the sun too long," said Mother. "The sun will burn your skin."

"I do not feel too hot," said Dave. And he went on playing in the sand.

Soon Mother called Dave to lunch. Dave's skin was red. It began to hurt.

"Oh, Mother," said Dave. "I stayed out in the sun too long. Look how red my skin is. And it hurts."

Mother rubbed oil on Dave's skin.

"My skin feels better now," said Dave. "I will not stay out in the sun too long again. I do not want the sun to burn my skin."

Summer Care of the Skin

Stay out in the sun only a little while every day. Then your skin will get used to the sunshine. The sun will make your skin brown, but it will not burn your skin. The sunshine is good for you. It helps your skin to make the sunshine vitamin. But too long a time in the sun will hurt your skin.

Winter Care of the Skin

Sometimes in the winter your skin will get dry and red. Rubbing cold cream on your skin will make it feel better. Cold cream keeps the skin soft.

Dry your skin carefully after washing. If you let your skin stay wet, it may get dry and hard.

The Story of Helen

There was once a little girl named Helen. When she was a baby she was very sick. After she got well, her mother found that something had happened to Helen.

Some of her doorways were closed. She could not see. She could not hear. And because she could not hear sounds, she did not learn how to speak.

Everyone thought that she could never learn anything. They thought that she would never grow up as other children do.

But one doorway was still open. It was the doorway of touch in her skin. She could feel with her fingers.

So a teacher began to teach Helen. She showed her how to spell words with her fingers, and to feel the teacher's hand when she spelled words. Did you ever see a person spell words with his fingers?

When Helen was older she learned to feel the mouth of a person who was speaking. After a while Helen learned to speak, but she could not hear what she was saying.

The little girl who had the closed doorways grew up to be a fine woman. She could talk to people. She wrote books. She had many friends.

Are you glad to have all five of your doorways?

What Have You Learned?

1. What words in the box finish the sentences in the list? *Do not write in the book.*

> *a.* if you get something in it
> *b.* out of a cut
> *c.* to keep your eyes clean
> *d.* too hard
> *e.* into your nose
> *f.* burn your skin
> *g.* after you eat
> *h.* into your ears

Never put your fingers __?__.
Do not put sharp things __?__.
Wash dirt __?__.
Do not rub your eye __?__.
Do not blow your nose __?__.
Tears help __?__.
The sun may __?__.
Brush your teeth __?__.

2. The five doorways to your body are your

        Eyes   Ears   Nose
           Mouth   Skin

Through which doorway do these things go?

  a. Good things to eat.
  b. The feel of the cold wind.
  c. The smell of good food.
  d. The color of a flower.
  e. The sound of music.
  f. The feel of the warm sunshine.
  g. A drink of water.
  h. A bonfire.
  i. Some one calling you to come out to play.
  j. The smell of a flower.
  k. The singing of birds.
  l. Your mother's face.

UNIT VIII

Health and Sleep

Seven to Seven

The second-grade room had a big clock upon the wall. One day Miss Smith saw Harry looking very hard at the clock.

"Miss Smith," said Harry, "the hands of the clock just keep going around and around."

"Yes, Harry," said Miss Smith, "the big hand goes around the clock every hour. The little hand goes from one number to the next number in an hour. It takes twelve hours for the little hand to go all around the clock."

"Now I know what the doctor wanted me to do" Harry said.

"What did he tell you to do?" asked Miss Smith.

"When I had a cold the doctor came to see me," said Harry. "He talked to Mother, and I heard him say that I ought to sleep all around the clock. Then I said that I ought to sleep in my bed, and not on a clock."

"Oh, yes," said Miss Smith, "the doctor wanted the hands of the clock to go all around the face of the clock while you were sleeping."

"Yes," said Dick. "But how long would that be?"

"Who can tell Dick how many hours the doctor wanted Harry to sleep?" asked Miss Smith.

"When does Harry go to sleep?" asked Mary.

"I go to sleep at seven," said Harry.

"Then if the little hand went all around the clock," said Dick, "it would be back at seven again."

"Yes," said Miss Smith. "How many hours would that take?"

The children looked hard at the numbers on the clock. They were counting.

"It would take twelve hours," said Dick.

"That is right," said Miss Smith. "The doctor wanted Harry to get twelve hours of sleep every night. Twelve hours of sleep every night will help to keep a boy or girl well and happy."

Something to Remember
Seven to Seven

Sleeping and Growing

Little babies sleep almost all the time. When a little baby is not sleeping, he is eating. He sleeps and he eats. That is why he grows so fast. His work is to grow. He can do this best if he just sleeps and eats.

When a baby can sit up or walk, he has many things to learn. He can not sleep all the time if he is to learn. But he still sleeps all night, and he sleeps every afternoon. He is still growing much faster than you are.

When you go to school, you have much to learn. You can't sleep in the afternoon. But you are still growing fast. You must eat good food, and you must get plenty of sleep. You ought to get some rest every day, too.

The older you get, the less you grow each year. That is why grown-ups need less sleep than you do. Now you need twelve hours of sleep a night.

Next year you will need a little less. The year after that, still a little less. When you are grown up, you will need about eight hours of sleep a night. You will not be growing then.

Now you are still growing. You need twelve hours of sleep a night to help you to grow.

Monkey Faces

"Good morning," said Mr. Strong, the principal.

"Good morning, good morning," said the children. They were always glad to see their principal.

Mr. Strong talked to Miss Smith. As he went out, he turned to the children.

"I am glad that there are no monkey faces in the second grade," he said.

"Why do you say that?" asked Miss Smith.

"Do you know what I sometimes see when I come into a room?" said Mr. Strong. "I see boys and girls making faces. I call them 'monkey faces.'"

The children looked at Mr. Strong. Then they looked at Miss Smith.

The principal smiled at them.

"You don't know what monkey faces are, do you?" he asked. "Well, did you ever see a boy open his mouth like this?"

And Mr. Strong opened his mouth in the biggest yawn you ever saw.

How the children laughed! Now they knew what Mr. Strong called a monkey face.

"I don't like to see boys and girls making faces," said Mr. Strong. "I don't like to see them yawning. Do you know why they do it?"

The second grade did not know.

"It's because they did not get enough good sleep the night before," said Mr. Strong. "No children should be yawning in school. If they get enough good sleep, they will not make faces; will they, Miss Smith?"

"Oh, no," said Miss Smith. "And you will not find the boys and girls of the second grade yawning, Mr. Strong."

"We all have the seven-to-seven habit," said Harry.

"Yes," said Mary, "everybody in this grade tries to sleep from seven at night to seven in the morning."

"That is fine," said Mr. Strong. "Now I will tell you another good thing that every one of you should remember.

The more quiet you keep,
The more quickly to sleep.

"Play quiet games before going to bed. Have your mother read you some stories before you go to bed."

"My mother says that it is best for me to go to picture shows in the afternoons," said Ruth. "She says that if I go in the evening, I will not sleep so well."

"Your mother is right," said Mr. Strong. "Afternoon is better than evening for picture shows. The more quiet you keep, the more quickly to sleep.

"And now there is one more thing I want you to remember when you go to sleep.

    Fresh air all around
    Will make you sleep sound."

"When I go to bed," said Bob, "my mother puts the window up from the bottom and down from the top. She says that is the way to let the fresh air in."

"Your mother is right, Bob," said Mr. Strong. "Fresh air is one of the things that keep you well and happy."

Here are Three Good Things to Remember
1. Sleep from seven to seven.
2. The more quiet you keep, the more quickly to sleep.
3. Fresh air all around will make you sleep sound.

Something to Talk About
Is it harder to get plenty of sleep in the city or in the country? Why?

Going to Bed

After supper Dan brushed his teeth up and down, inside and outside. Then he remembered to hang up his toothbrush.

Soon it was time to go to bed.

"Mother," said Dan, "I learned something at school today."

"Don't you learn something at school every day?" asked Mother.

"Oh, yes," laughed Dan. "But today Mr. Strong, our principal, told us two things about sleeping."

"Do you remember them?" asked Mother. "You always try to 'Sleep from seven to seven.' What new things did you learn?"

"The first one was, 'The more quiet you keep, the more quickly to sleep,'" said Dan.

"I like that one," said Mother. "Taking a warm bath before going to bed is a good way to make you quiet and to help you to sleep well. Your bath is all ready for you, Dan. And here are some clean night clothes."

"Good," Dan said. "I like to take a bath. I will put this underwear in the wash. Tomorrow morning I shall put on clean underwear. Then I shall be all clean to go to school."

Dan climbed into the tub of warm water. He carefully washed his neck and ears with soap. He washed under his arms and all over his body.

"Mother," said Dan, "I can not remember what the other thing was that Mr. Strong told us to do."

"Well," said Mother, "maybe you will remember soon."

Dan got into his bed, and Mother covered him up.

"It feels so good to be clean," said Dan. "And now maybe I can sleep all around the clock."

"Good night," said Mother. She opened the windows a little from the top and a little from the bottom.

"Oh," said Dan, sitting up in bed. "Now I remember. 'Fresh air all around will make you sleep sound.'"

What Have You Learned?

1. Do little babies sleep almost all the time?

2. Is eight hours every night enough sleep for you?

3. Is eight hours every night enough sleep for your father and mother?

4. Should you play quiet games just before bedtime?

5. Is it good for you to go to picture shows in the evening?

6. Does plenty of sleep help you to grow and keep well?

7. Is it a good thing to put your clothes on the floor?

8. Is a warm bath bad for you just before you go to bed?

9. Should you have plenty of fresh air while you sleep?

10. Should you change underwear often?

Stop and Think

Do You Do These Things?

Tell how many of these Good Bedtime Health Habits you have.

1. I brush my teeth after supper.
2. I go to the toilet.
3. I wash my hands and feet.
4. I wash my face and my ears and my neck.
5. I take off my clothes and hang them up over a chair.
6. Twice a week I take a bath with warm water and soap.
7. I put on clean night clothes.
8. I open the window from the top and bottom.
9. I go to sleep in a clean bed.

UNIT IX

More Good Habits

Sport

"Oh, Miss Smith," said Jack. "My dog, Sport, has learned to sit up."

"How did you teach him to sit up, Jack?" asked Miss Smith.

"I put Sport's supper on a plate," said Jack. "But I would not give it to him then. I would put Sport in a corner and say, 'Sit up.'"

"Did he sit up?" asked Tom.

"No," said Jack, "he could not do it at first. But I would take his front feet in my hand. I would put his back to the wall. Then I would say, 'Sit up, Sport.' I would hold him that way in the corner. After that I would feed him his supper.

"I did that every evening for a week. Pretty soon Sport could sit up by himself. Now every time Sport is hungry, he sits up."

"That is how I learned to stand on my head," said Fred. "I had to stand on my head in the corner first. But I never had to learn to sit up, did I?"

"Yes," said Miss Smith, "you had to learn to sit up and to stand up, Fred. But that was long ago. You can not remember about it now."

Walking Habits

"My baby sister can stand up," said Tom. "And she is learning to walk. She holds on to my hand. It is hard for her to walk. Sometimes she falls down."

"Walking is a habit that we have to learn, too," said Fred.

"That is so," said Miss Smith. "Standing, walking, and sitting are habits that we learn. Pretty soon Tom's baby sister will learn these habits. We must be careful that all the habits we learn are good ones."

"Baby walks with her feet too far from each other," said Tom.

Miss Smith laughed.

"Baby will learn to walk right as she keeps on," she said. "Then her feet will be near each other. But you must see that she learns to point her feet straight ahead."

"I walk with my feet pointed straight ahead," said Harry.

"That is the thing to do," said Miss Smith. "You will hurt your feet if you don't. Remember to point your feet straight ahead when you walk."

Sitting Habits

"Some boys are bigger outside the room than inside," said Miss Smith.

The boys looked at each other.

"The girls are just as big inside the room as outside," said Miss Smith.

The girls smiled at each other.

"Look at Larry," said Miss Smith. "See what a little boy he is now. His head is not nearly so high as Martha's."

Larry sat straight up at his desk.

"Oh," said Miss Smith. "That was my mistake. I see that Larry is really as big as Martha."

All the children laughed.

"Then there is another thing," said Miss Smith, as she walked between the rows of desks.

"Here is a little girl with only one leg. Here is another, and another."

There was a noise as all the girls put both feet on the floor. Some of them had been sitting on one foot.

"That was a mistake, too," said Miss Smith. "Now all our girls really have two feet."

The children laughed again.

"There is still another thing I am thinking about," said Miss Smith. "I do wish we all had good strong backs. Some backs just can't hold the children up. The poor children have to rest on their desks. I wish that we all had strong backs."

All at once many children sat up very straight.

"My, my," said Miss Smith, "those backs are really strong! My boys and girls do not need desks to rest on. That was another mistake I made."

Now all the children were sitting up straight and tall in their seats.

"Well, now," said Miss Smith. "We all are tall and straight with two feet on the floor. Can't we stay that way?"

"Yes, yes," said the second grade.

Things to Look For

1. Which of the children in the picture have good sitting habits?

2. Do the children in your room have good sitting habits?

3. Which children in the picture have good standing or walking habits?

4. Watch the children coming to your school. See how many have good habits of standing or walking.

5. Do you have good habits of sitting, standing, and walking?

UNIT X

Always Be Careful

An Automobile on the Sidewalk

Officer Dennis had come to school to talk to the children. Officer Dennis often stood at the street corner. He told the line of automobiles when to stop and when to go. He had come to talk to the children about it.

"Now," said Officer Dennis, "did you ever see an automobile coming down the sidewalk?"

The second-grade children looked at Officer Dennis. Then they looked at each other. They had never seen an automobile on the sidewalk.

"They don't know what you mean, Mr. Dennis," said Miss Smith.

"I mean just what I said," said Officer Dennis. "Did you ever see any one driving an automobile on the sidewalk? Why not? It ought to be a good place to drive an automobile."

"But a sidewalk is not the place for an automobile," said Mary. "The street is the place for automobiles."

"The sidewalk is for people," said Bob. "They should not be in the street."

"Yes," said Officer Dennis. "The street is for automobiles and the sidewalk for people. Is that right?"

"Yes," said all the children.

"Then why is it that sometimes I see children in the street?" asked Officer Dennis. "Where did you say that people belong?"

Officer Dennis looked at Jim.

"Oh, oh, — on the sidewalk," said Jim. He was so surprised that he could hardly talk.

"On the sidewalk," said Officer Dennis. "Let us remember that. Automobiles on the street. People on the sidewalk. And each one should keep where he belongs."

Bob put up his hand. Officer Dennis nodded to him.

"But we can't stay on the sidewalk all the time," said Bob. "We should never get home from school if we did. There are streets all around the school. If we could not cross the streets, we should have to stay here."

All the children laughed. Officer Dennis laughed, too.

"Well," he said, "you don't want to stay at school all night. We have to get you home in some way. But the streets belong to the automobiles. So what can we do about it?"

Officer Dennis turned to look at Alice.

"That is why we have safety-patrol boys," said Alice. "They help us to get across the streets."

"That's right," said Officer Dennis. "That is why we have safety-patrol boys. And how do safety-patrol boys help? They wait until no automobiles are coming. Then they let you cross the street. They hold up their hands and you can cross. But then a car comes. The patrol boy puts down his hands. Now the street belongs to the cars again. You don't belong there."

"I am glad that we have safety-patrol boys to help us across the street safely," said Mary.

"Yes," said Officer Dennis. "And I help you to get across the street downtown. I stand at a place where one street crosses another street. When I stop the line of cars on one street, the line of cars on the other street goes across. First I let the cars on one street go. Then I let the cars on the other street go."

"When do the people cross?" Bob asked.

"The people walk across the street when I let the cars go across that street," said Officer Dennis. "They wait on the sidewalk when cars are going along the street they want to cross."

"When I go downtown, I'll watch the policeman," said Jim. "I'll cross just when he tells me to cross."

"Fine," said Officer Dennis, "but there is another thing. No jaywalking. Jaywalking means walking across a street when cars are going along that street. Jaywalking is dangerous. You might be hurt by a car."

"I ran into the street after a ball once," said Mary. "A car that was driving by almost ran over me."

"I guess it did," said Officer Dennis. "The drivers don't expect you to do that. Do you see how that is? The street belongs to the automobiles. The drivers go right along. All at once you run out into the road in front of them. They don't expect to see you there. Maybe they can't stop."

"It surprises them," said Bob.

"Of course it does. But the biggest surprise is when cars are standing at the side of the street. Then maybe you come out from between those cars. First, the driver can't see you. Then you are right in front of him. That is a very bad thing to do. Never run out between cars."

"I'll never do that," said Bob.

"Good," said Officer Dennis. "Now you know all about crossing streets. No automobiles on the sidewalk. No children in the street. Then you can't get hurt."

Officer Dennis nodded.

"Now I'll have to say good-by," he said.

"Good-by, good-by," said the second grade.

Officer Dennis nodded again.

"I have been glad to see you," he said. "I expect to see you downtown some time. Just call out 'Hello.'"

What Have You Learned?

Find the right word or words to finish each sentence. *Do not write in the book.*

1. The place for automobiles is __?__.
    the street   the sidewalk
2. The place for people is __?__.
    the street   the sidewalk
3. Patrol boys help children to get across the streets __?__.
    around the school   downtown
4. The place to cross a street is __?__.
    where a street crosses another street
    between places where streets cross
5. The time to cross a street is __?__.
    when the policeman stops the cars on that street
    when cars are going along that street
6. If we come to a place where lights tell us when to cross the street, we cross when the light is __?__.
    red   green   yellow

Playing Is Lots of Fun

The boys and girls of the second grade liked to play games. They liked to play at home. They liked to play at school.

One day Jack hurt his leg when he was playing. The doctor fixed Jack's leg. But Jack had to stay in bed until his leg was well. He could not go to school. He could not play. The boys and girls of the second grade were very sorry for Jack.

At last Jack came back to school. Everybody was glad to see him. And how glad Jack was to be back!

"Playing is lots of fun," said Jack, "but I do not like to get hurt. When you are hurt you miss playing with your friends. And if you can't come to school you miss your work."

The Safe Play Club

"You are right, Jack," said Miss North, the school nurse. "We don't like to get hurt. Just think of all the good times you missed while you were in bed. And think of all the money it took to have your leg fixed. Boys and girls should play. But their play should be safe play."

"Let us have a Safe Play Club," said Jack.

"Oh, that would be fun!" said Helen.

"That will be a good club to have," said Miss North.

All the boys and girls wanted to be members of the Safe Play Club.

"We will have our first meeting next week," said Miss North. "All the members of the Safe Play Club will keep their eyes open. They will find out

>How we can play safely.
>Where we can play safely."

The Meeting of the Safe Play Club

Miss North started the meeting of the club. "We will now have reports on how we can play safely," said Miss North. "Helen, what have you to report this week?"

Helen stood up tall and straight. She read from a paper.

"Miss North and members of the Safe Play Club," she began. "I have seen some bad things on our school playground at recess. I do not think they should have happened.

"Charles is in the first grade. He was playing in the sand. He began to throw sand, and it got into Rita's eyes. Miss North had to get the sand out of Rita's eyes. It hurt her. And Rita's eyes were very red. Her mother had to take her to a doctor. I do not think that we should ever throw sand.

"William was having fun throwing stones. One of the stones hit Susan and hurt her. Susan did not cry. William was sorry he had hurt Susan. He said that he would not throw stones any more."

"That is a good report, Helen," said Miss North. "And now I am going to call on Tom for his report."

Tom stood on both feet with his hands at his sides. He stood up straight and tall.

"Miss North and members of the Safe Play Club," he said, "I think fast running on the school ground is dangerous. The big boys run too fast.

"I asked them please not to run where the little children wanted to play. The little children might get hurt. 'Safe Play' means Always Be Careful."

"That is right, Tom," said Miss North. "'Safe Play' means Always Be Careful."

Where to Play

"Now," said Miss North, "who can tell us where we can play safely? Can the members of the Safe Play Club think of places where it is safe to play?"

"The playground at our school is a safe place to play," said Mary. "That is, it will be safe if everybody remembers *how* to play."

"My back yard is a safe place to play," said Peter. "No automobiles can hurt me if I play in my back yard. But you can't play baseball there. You might break a window."

"The playground is a good place to play," said Billy. "It is big enough for two games of baseball at once. And you can not break any windows if you play baseball there."

"Once I went to a big city," said Alice. "There were no back yards or playgrounds for the children to play in. So the policeman had put up a sign in the street. It said, 'Play Street.' No automobiles went on that street. Then the children could have a safe place to play."

Miss North smiled. "We want all children to have a safe place to play," she said. "And we want all children to know how to play. Remember that 'Safe Play' means Always Be Careful."

"That is what we will try to do," said the members of the Safe Play Club. "Always be careful."

"Oh," laughed Alice. "We are all members of the A B C Club — Always Be Careful. When we are playing together, we can say A B C."

Miss North laughed. "Members of the Safe Play Club, we have had a fine meeting. And remember A B C."

The White Box

Jim had seen a little white box in the bathroom. He did not know what was in the white box. One day he found out.

Jim was making a toy dog for the baby. He was sawing the dog out of wood. Father had given him a saw for his birthday. It was fun to saw.

Jim was going to color the toy dog yellow. He knew that the baby would like a yellow dog.

Then Jim sawed his finger. He did not cut it badly, but blood ran over his hand. Some of the blood got on the little toy dog. Jim called his father.

"Well," said Father, "I see that you need to be fixed up. Let us go to the bathroom and wash the cut."

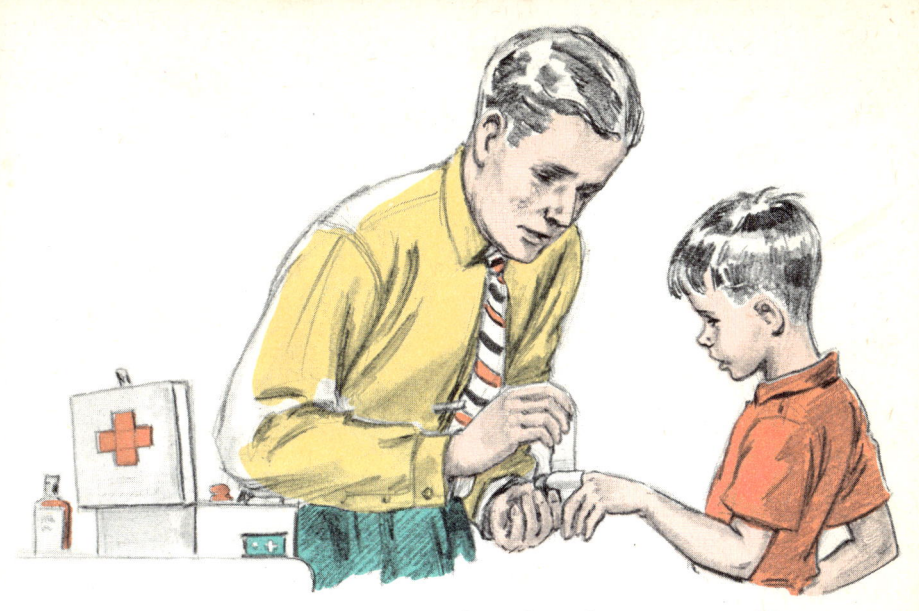

So they went to the bathroom. Jim washed the cut with soap and water. Father got down the white box.

"Here is the First Aid Kit," he said. "Let us fix that cut."

Soon Jim had a bandage on his finger. He did not cry.

"You are a good boy," said Father.

"Now I'll go back and make that toy dog for baby," said Jim. "And I will keep my fingers away from the saw."

Jim's First Aid Kit

Jim brought the white box to school. "This is a First Aid Kit," said Jim. "My father says that everybody ought to have a First Aid Kit. You never know when you might get hurt."

Miss Smith took the white box and showed it to the second grade.

"Aid means to give help," she said. "First aid is what we have to do first to help a person who has been hurt. The things in this little white box may be used to give first aid for little cuts."

Then she showed the children everything in the white box.

"The blood will often clean a cut. But here is soap so that you can wash a cut clean of dirt. Here are scissors to cut the bandage and the tape.

"This is iodine. Have Mother put iodine on the cut after you have washed the cut carefully.

"This bandage," she said, "is all rolled up and covered so that dirt cannot get on it.

"This tape is to put on over the bandage. On one side of the tape is something that sticks. The tape will hold the bandage in place.

"There is everything in the little white box to aid you if you get cut."

"Yes," said Jim. "And the box has directions on the outside which tell you just what you ought to do if you get cut."

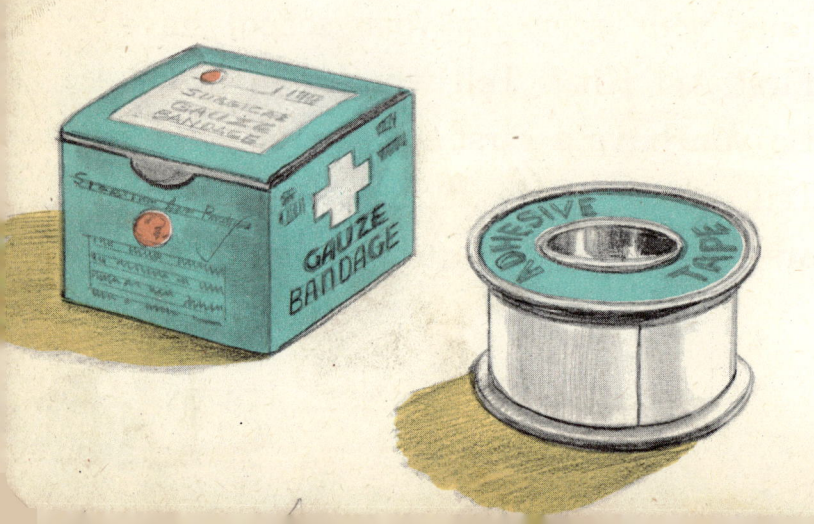

Miss Smith read the directions.

Directions

1. Wash the cut with warm water and soap.
2. Have some one put iodine on the cut.
3. Put a clean bandage over the cut when the iodine is dry to keep out all dirt.
4. Put a piece of tape over the bandage to hold it in place.

The second grade thought that a First Aid Kit was a very fine thing to have.

Things to Talk About

Does your room or your school have a First Aid Kit? Tell what is in it.

Do you have a First Aid Kit at home?

Tell what you would do if you cut yourself.

What Have You Learned?

Find in the box the words that finish the sentences. *Do not write in the book.*

---

a. dangerous   *d.* stones   *f.* baseball
b. windows   *e.* careful   *g.* safe
c. eyes

---

1. Throwing sand may hurt people's __?__.

2. We should never throw __?__.

3. Fast running is __?__.

4. Playing ball in some places may break __?__.

5. The playground is the place to play __?__.

6. The street is a __?__ place to play only at a time when it is shut off from automobiles.

7. Safe play means to be always __?__.

VOCABULARY

The vocabulary of *The Health Parade* has been carefully selected in order to hold reading difficulty to a minimum. A list of 492 words was assumed as known. Of these assumed words, 396 are from the Core Vocabulary for Grade Two, a list of words based on an extensive study of reading materials for the first grade and therefore likely to be known to children entering the second grade. The remaining 96 words of the assumed list (as well as many of the 396) occur in *Spick and Span*, the first book of this series.

In addition to the assumed words, 190 new words have been introduced gradually. No more than three new words appear on any page, and every new word is used a minimum of three times. All variants were counted as new words except those formed by the addition of -s, -es, -'s, -s', -d, -ed, -ing, -er, -est, -ly, -y, -n, and un-. All compounds except those formed by combining *some*, *every*, or *any* with *thing*, *one*, *body*, *self*, or *times* were considered new words and treated as such. Proper names were not included in this vocabulary control. The following list includes the new words by pages.

viii. habits
1. log
   cabin
   smell
2. can't
   without
3. lamp
   pump
4. list
5. harms
6. driver
7. slowed
   between
   meals
8. screened
   porch
10. dining
11. kitchen
    stove
12. it's
    furnace
    fireplace
13. twice
15. both
    same
    stood
16. forgot
    hooks
17. bathroom
18. outdoor
    washcloth
    washbasin
19. faucet
    bucket
    course
20. cup
    pour
21. wall
    set
22. row
    helpers
23. -self
24. feel
    card
    remember
25. finish
    sentences
27. blackberries
28. toast
    flies
    bugs
29. cocoa
30. vitamins
    sunshine
    exercise
32. spinach
34. salad
36. tomorrow
37. sunbath
38. skin
    straight
    bones
40. beef
    quart
41. soup
    chocolate
42. kept
43. nice
44. second
    wrote
45. beans
    lettuce
47. tongue
    short
    thermometer

183

49. indoors
    above
51. raincoat
    umbrella
52. sick
    change
53. automobile
    point
54. poem
    north
55. overshoes
    body
    heat
56. suit
    cooler
57. bodies
58. clothing
62. coughs
63. valentine
    hearts
64. secret
    kerchoo
    maybe
65. germs
66. happened
    yesterday
68. whispering
    circle
71. sorry
75. quickly
76. apron
77. plenty
78. ago
    often
82. manners
84. excuse
86. I'll
87. fork
    spoon

    teach
88. that's
    you're
89. closed
90. tall
    pieces
    plate
94. tonight
    tablecloth
    knives
95. roast
    family
96. napkins
97. enjoy
99. meet
102. doorways
108. aid
    tears
109. break
    throw
    sand
110. music
    sounds
    hit
111. camp
112. bonfire
    lots
    'way
114. bleed
119. alcohol
121. seashore
124. speak
125. spell
    ever
    person
129. clock
130. number
    ought

133. afternoon
134. less
    eight
135. monkey
    principal
137. yawn
138. quiet
    evening
142. underwear
144. bedtime
147. corner
150. ahead
151. desk
    mistake
    really
157. sidewalk
    officer
    line
158. mean
    driving
159. belong
160. nodded
162. downtown
163. jaywalking
    dangerous
164. expect
167. fixed
168. club
169. members
170. reports
    playground
173. baseball
176. blood
177. kit
    bandage
179. tape
    iodine
180. directions

PRINTED IN THE UNITED STATES OF AMERICA